Hot Air Balloons

Volume

Dianne Irving

Publishing Credits

Editor
Sara Johnson

Editorial Director
Dona Herweck Rice

Editor-in-Chief
Sharon Coan, M.S.Ed.

Creative Director
Lee Aucoin

Publisher
Rachelle Cracchiolo, M.S.Ed.

Image Credits

The author and publisher would like to gratefully credit or acknowledge the following for permission to reproduce copyright material: cover Shutterstock; p.1 Photolibrary.com; pp.4, 5 Photolibrary.com/Mary Evans Picture Library; p.6 Photolibrary.com; p.7 (top) Getty Images; (bottom) Shutterstock; p.8 Shutterstock; p.9 Photolibrary.com; p.10 Shutterstock (background), Big Stock; p.11 Photolibrary.com; p.12 iStockphotos; p.13 Photolibrary.com; p.14 Shutterstock; p.14 (inset) Photolibrary.com; p.15 Shutterstock; p.16 Alamy; p.17 Photolibray.com/Alamy; pp.22,23 Getty Images; pp.24–25 Corbis; pp.26, 27 Alamy; p.28; Dallas Aquarium

Illustrations on pp. 18–21 by Bruce Rankin

While every care has been taken to trace and acknowledge copyright, the publishers tender their apologies for any accidental infringement where copyright has proved untraceable. They would be pleased to come to a suitable arrangement with the rightful owner in each case.

Teacher Created Materials

5301 Oceanus Drive
Huntington Beach, CA 92649-1030
http://www.tcmpub.com

ISBN 978-0-7439-0920-4
© 2009 Teacher Created Materials, Inc.
Reprinted 2010
Printed in China

Table of Contents

First Flights

Did you know that the first passengers in a hot air balloon were animals? A sheep, a duck, and a rooster were carried in a basket attached to the balloon. This balloon flight took place in 1783 in France. The Montgolfier (mont-GOHL-fih-uhr) brothers, Joseph and Étienne (eh-TEE-en), made the balloon from paper and **linen**.

A crowd watches the first passengers in a hot air balloon—a sheep, a duck, and a rooster.

Volume and Capacity

Volume is the amount of space that a 3-D object takes up. How much **matter** a 3-D object holds is known as capacity (kuh-PASS-uh-tee). Sometimes, capacity is known as "inside volume."

This painting shows the first hot air balloon flight carrying humans. The humans stood in a large basket below the hot air balloon.

A few months later, the Montgolfier brothers tried out a balloon with human passengers. Two men flew over Paris, France. This balloon was the first **aircraft** to take people into the sky.

The Right Fuel

The first hot air balloons were powered by fire. The Montgolfier brothers believed it was the smoke that lifted the balloon into the air. But they soon discovered that hot air, not smoke, pushed the balloon upward.

It did not take long for people to realize there were problems with lighting fires in the hot air balloon baskets. Sparks could reach the balloon and set it on fire. **Balloonists** (buh-LOON-ists) needed a safer way to create hot air.

LET'S EXPLORE MATH

Some balloon baskets are prisms. To find out the volume of a prism, multiply its length by its width by its height: Volume can be measured in cubic inches (in.³) and cubic feet (ft.³).

This prism has a volume of 36 cubic inches.

height = 3 in.
width = 2 in.
length = 6 in.

length × width × height = Volume
6 in. × 2 in. × 3 in. = 36 in.³

Use the volume **formula** to find the volume of the balloon baskets below. Use the given dimensions:

a. length = 4 ft., width = 6 ft., height = 5 ft.

b. length = 6 ft., width = 8 ft., height = 4 ft.

In the 1930s, balloons were filled with gas. **Hydrogen** (high-druh-juhn) and **helium** (HEE-lee-uhm) gas are lighter than air. They make balloons float upward.

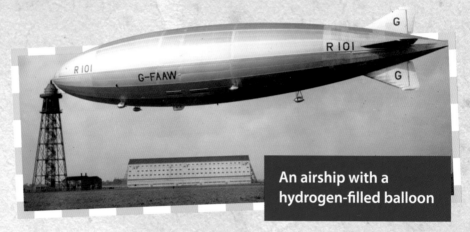

An airship with a hydrogen-filled balloon

In the 1960s, a **propane** burner was invented that filled the balloons with hot air. The burner was fixed above the basket, just under the large opening of the balloon. The flame was small and did not create sparks. It was a safe way to heat the air. This type of burner is still used today.

A propane burner in a hot air balloon

Bad Gas

Hydrogen gas is not very safe. It is highly **flammable** (FLAM-uh-buhl). Explosions easily occured in balloons filled with hydrogen. Balloonists stopped using the gas.

How Does It Work?

A hot air balloon is a special bag filled with hot air. A balloon rises because the hot air inside it is lighter than the colder air outside. One cubic foot of air weighs about 1 ounce (28 g), but 1 cubic foot of *hot* air only weighs about ¾ of an ounce (21 g).

The hot air inside a balloon will carry the balloon high in the sky.

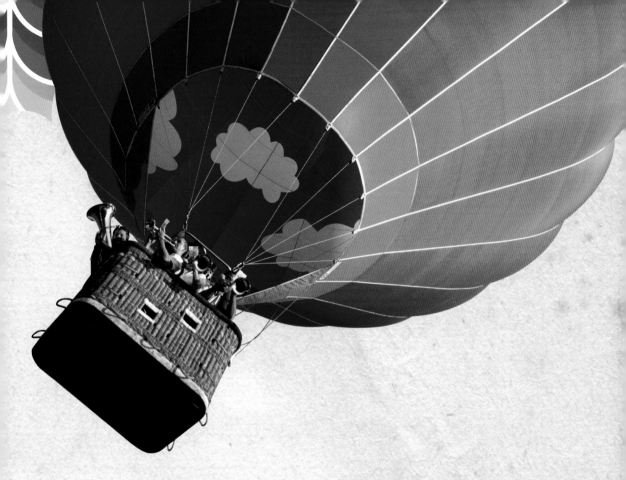

A hot air balloon must be big. It has to contain enough hot air to carry its basket, the pilot, and any passengers. The size of the balloon depends on the weight that it has to carry. The heavier the load, the bigger the balloon must be. This means that the balloon's volume gets larger as the weight of the load gets larger.

Passenger Balloons

A balloon needs a volume of at least 60,000 cubic feet (about 1,700 m^3) to carry 2 passengers. Most balloons that are able to carry 3 or 4 people have a volume of 100,000 cubic feet (about 2,832 m^3).

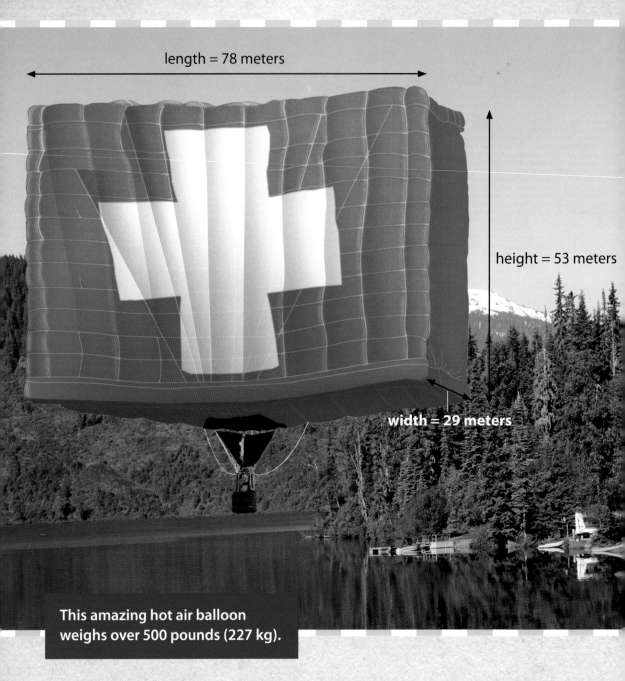

length = 78 meters

height = 53 meters

width = 29 meters

This amazing hot air balloon weighs over 500 pounds (227 kg).

The bag of the balloon is called the envelope. The envelope's opening is called the "mouth." Today, most envelopes are a light-bulb shape. But some are unusual shapes such as houses, animals, or even flags.

The envelope is made of **nylon** (NIGH-lon). Balloons have a **sensor** that gives information to the pilot about the temperature inside the envelope. The pilot uses this information to check if the envelope is getting too hot. If the temperature gets too high, the nylon could melt.

A temperature sensor

LET'S EXPLORE MATH

Use the dimensions shown on the flag hot air balloon on page 10 to find the volume of the balloon's envelope.

Getting Around

The pilot of a hot air balloon controls how high the balloon flies. This is done by turning the burner's flame up and down. Turning *up* the flame makes the air inside the envelope warmer. This causes the balloon to **ascend**. Turning *down* the flame makes the air inside the envelope cooler. This causes the balloon to **descend**.

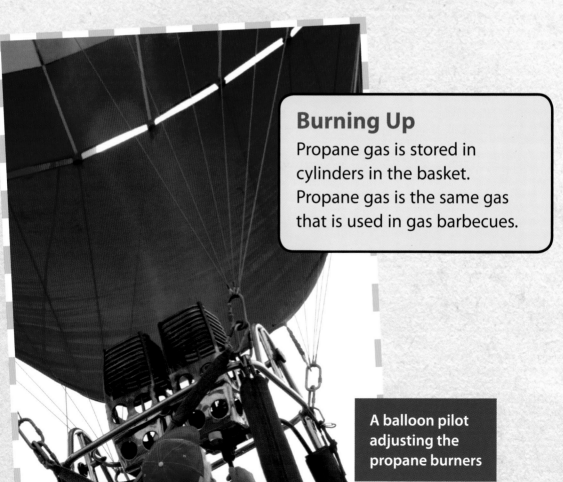

Burning Up

Propane gas is stored in cylinders in the basket. Propane gas is the same gas that is used in gas barbecues.

A balloon pilot adjusting the propane burners

This balloon pilot is taking a map with him on his flight.

The pilot can use the wind to move sideways. The wind moves in different directions at different **altitudes**. The pilot moves the balloon up and down to find winds that help it move in the right direction. The pilot studies weather **forecasts** before flying to find out the wind directions on the day of the flight.

The amount of heat needed to lift a balloon depends on the air temperature outside the envelope. The air inside the envelope needs to be warmer than the air outside it. This is why many balloon flights take place in the cool, early morning. There is also less wind then, so it is easier to control the balloon.

In the Basket
The basket is usually made of a material called **wicker**. When the balloon lands, the wicker basket hits the ground without breaking or bouncing too much.

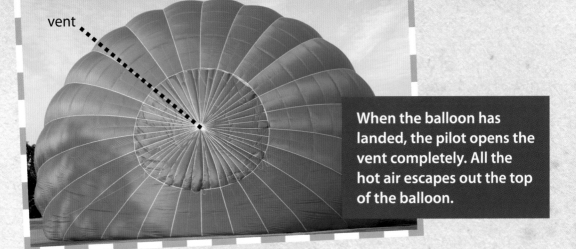

vent

When the balloon has landed, the pilot opens the vent completely. All the hot air escapes out the top of the balloon.

The pilot can open a vent to let cool air into the envelope. This helps bring the balloon down. The vent is a flap of material at the top of the balloon. It opens and closes with a cord. It is used to make the balloon descend very quickly.

LET'S EXPLORE MATH

When you know the volume, length, and width of a prism, you can find its height. The formula to use is: Volume ÷ (length × width) = height.

The volume of the prism below is 48 ft.³ Figure out its height using the formula below and the information in the diagram. *Hint*: Remember to work out the part of the equation in the parentheses first.

$$\underset{\text{Volume}}{\underline{\hspace{1.5cm}}} \div (\underset{\text{length}}{\underline{\hspace{1cm}}} \times \underset{\text{width}}{\underline{\hspace{1cm}}}) = \underset{\text{height}}{\underline{\hspace{1cm}}}$$

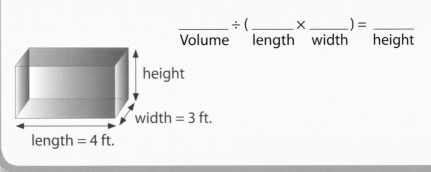

height

width = 3 ft.

length = 4 ft.

Taking Off

Balloons get off the ground in different ways. For some balloons, the pilot and passengers use a small step ladder and climb into an upright basket. For others, the balloon, the basket, and the people in it lie on their sides. A large fan blows air into the mouth of the balloon. When the balloon is half **inflated** (in-FLAY-tuhd), the pilot starts the burner. The flames heat the air inside the envelope. As the air heats up, the balloon rises and pulls the basket upright.

A fan blows air into the mouth of the balloon while the balloon passengers lie on their sides in the basket.

When the basket is upright, the pilot turns the burner up. As the flames heat the air inside the envelope, the basket lifts off the ground.

The balloon and its passengers ascend into the sky.

Helium Balloon Lift

You probably know about helium-filled balloons. You know how easily they float away. Think about the lifting power of helium-filled balloons. How many balloons do you think it would take to lift you off the ground?

Say you have a balloon with a **diameter** of 1 foot and a volume of .5 cubic feet (over 14,000 cm³). That volume is enough to lift half a slice of bread. A slice of bread weighs 1 ounce (28 g). That means it would take 2 balloons of this size to lift one slice of bread. In other words, 1 cubic foot of helium gas can lift 1 ounce.

It takes .5 cubic feet of helium to lift half a slice of bread.

There are 16 ounces in 1 pound. So, if 1 balloon can lift .5 of an ounce, you would need 32 helium-filled balloons of that size to lift 1 pound. That is quite a lot of balloons!

It takes 16 cubic feet of helium to lift 1 pound.

LET'S EXPLORE MATH

A balloon's wicker basket has the following measurements: 4 feet long, 4 feet wide, 5 feet high.

a. What is its volume?

One person takes up this much room in the basket: 2 feet in length, 2 feet in width, and 5 feet in height.

b. How many people can fit into the basket?
   Hint: You will need to work out the space that 1 person takes up first.

If you weigh 78 pounds, how much helium gas would it take to lift you? Remember you need 16 cubic feet of helium gas to lift 1 pound. So, you would need 1,248 cubic feet (35 m³) of helium gas to lift you. That means it would take 2,496 helium balloons to lift you if each balloon lifts .5 ounces. That really is a lot of balloons!

$$
\begin{array}{r}
^{4}\\
78 \text{ pounds}\\
\times\ \ 16 \text{ cubic feet}\\
\hline
^{1}\\
468\\
+\ 780\\
\hline
1{,}248 \text{ cubic feet}
\end{array}
$$

- - - - - - - - - -

2 balloons = 1 cubic foot

$$
\begin{array}{r}
^{1}\\
1{,}248 \text{ cubic feet}\\
\times\ \ \ \ 2 \text{ balloons per cubic foot}\\
\hline
2{,}496 \text{ balloons in total}
\end{array}
$$

Big Balloons

In 1836, a balloon called Le Géant (the Giant) was able to lift up to 4.5 tons (4 tonnes). That is about the same as 2 pick-up trucks! The balloon contained 200,000 cubic feet (5,663 m³) of helium gas.

1,248 cubic feet

Say you wanted to buy a single balloon big enough to lift you. What would be the volume of that one balloon? You would need a single balloon with a volume of 1,248 cubic feet (35 m³) to lift your weight of 78 pounds. The balloon would have a diameter of about 13 feet. That's an enormous balloon!

Balloon World Records

Since the earliest balloon flights, people have tried to set world records for hot air ballooning. Today, many of the record-breaking balloons use both hot air and gas to help them fly.

Dr. Vijaypat Singhania lifts off in his hot air balloon *Mission Impossible (MI-70K)* from Mumbai, India.

LET'S EXPLORE MATH

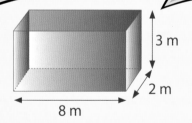

3 m

2 m

8 m

Many record hot air balloon flights have crossed over water. In metric measurement, 1 cubic meter (m³) holds 1,000 liters (L) of water.

Use the diagram of the prism to answer the questions below.

a. Figure out the volume of the prism.

b. Figure out how many liters of water it can hold.

c. Explain how you solved this problem.

The record for the quickest balloon flight around the world was set in 2002 by Steve Fossett. It took 320 hours and 33 minutes. This was also the first **solo** around-the-world balloon flight.

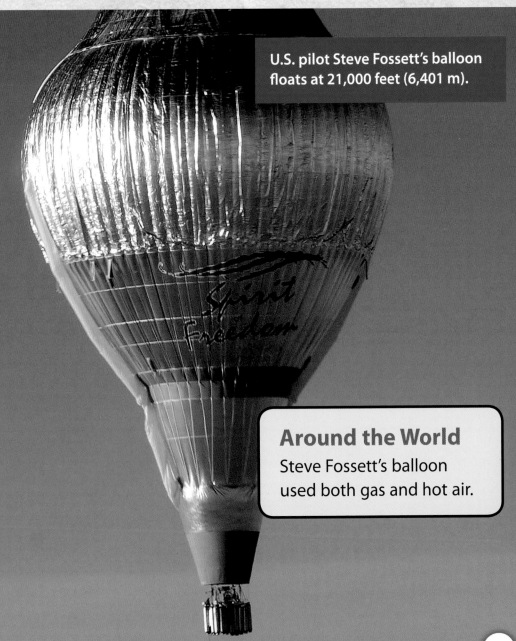

U.S. pilot Steve Fossett's balloon floats at 21,000 feet (6,401 m).

Around the World
Steve Fossett's balloon used both gas and hot air.

Balloon Flight Time Line

For more than 200 years, people have been making balloon flights. In the past 20 years, adventurers (ad-VEN-chur-ers) have set new challenges. Balloons have crossed oceans and traveled nonstop around the world.

1978

The *Double Eagle II* was the first balloon to cross the Atlantic Ocean. The balloon was filled with helium gas. Their trip took 137 hours.

1987

Richard Branson and Per Lindstrand crossed the Atlantic Ocean in a hot air balloon. They flew 2,900 miles (4,667 km) in 33 hours. The hot air balloon had a volume of 2.3 million cubic feet (65,129 m³). At the time, it was the largest hot air balloon ever flown.

Bertrand Piccard and Brian Jones fly high above the Swiss Alps in the *Breitling Orbiter 3* balloon.

1991

Richard Branson and Per Lindstrand were the first people to cross the Pacific Ocean in a hot air balloon. They flew 4,766 miles (7,670 km) in 47 hours.

2005

In 2005, Indian pilot Dr. Vijaypat Singhania became the first person to reach a height of 69,852 feet (21,290 m) above sea level in a hot air balloon.

1999

Bertrand Piccard and Brian Jones flew around the world in a hot air balloon without stopping. It took them 19 days, 21 hours, and 55 minutes to travel 29,055 miles (46,759 km).

Balloons for Fun

Today, many hot air balloons are used for fun. People take balloon rides and enter races. They can attend ballooning events.

Many countries hold hot air balloon festivals. These events are a great way for people to learn more about the sport of ballooning.

Hundreds and hundreds of balloons take part in hot air balloon festivals. They really are an amazing sight!

All hot air balloons must be big enough to carry the weight of their load. Different balloons carry different weights. Without a big enough envelope, some hot air balloons would never get off the ground!

LET'S EXPLORE MATH

When folded, a balloon envelope is 4 meters long, 2 meters wide, and 2 meters high.

a. What is the volume of this folded envelope?

These folded envelopes are packed into a container. The container is 8 meters long, 8 meters high, and 2 meters wide.

b. How many balloon envelopes will fit into 1 container this size?

c. How many balloon envelopes will fit into 15 containers this size?

A Fishy Problem

André owns his own business. He builds both large and small tanks for aquariums. He recently built some new tanks for Seaview Aquarium.

- Tank A is 6 feet long, 4 feet wide, and 5 feet high.

- Tank B is 15 feet long, 4 feet wide, and 2 feet high.

- Tank C is 8 meters long and 4 meters wide. It has a volume of 96 cubic meters.

Solve It!

a. What are the volumes of Tanks A and B?

b. What do you notice about the volumes of both tanks?

c. What is the height of Tank C?

d. How many liters of water does Tank C hold?

Use the steps below to help you answer the questions above.

Step 1: To solve question **a**, use the formula:
length × width × height = Volume

Step 2: To answer **b**, think about the dimensions of both Tanks A and B. *Hint*: Drawing a rectangular prism for each tank and marking the dimensions may help you.

Step 3: To solve question **c**, use the formula: Volume ÷ (length × width) = height. Remember to solve the part of the equation in the parentheses first.

Step 4: Use the volume of Tank C to figure out how many liters it holds. *Hint*: 1 cubic meter (1 m^3) holds 1,000 liters (L) of water.

Glossary

aircraft—machines that fly in the air

altitudes—heights

ascend—to go up

balloonists—people who fly balloons

descend—to go down

diameter—the distance across a circle

flammable—catches fire easily

forecasts—predictions about what something will be like

formula—a strategy or plan

helium—a light kind of gas that will not burn

hydrogen—a kind of gas

inflated—filled with air

linen—a kind of fabric woven from natural fibers

matter—a substance that takes up space

nylon—a very strong fabric made from artificial fibers

propane—a heavy kind of gas that is flammable

sensor—a machine that detects something

solo—single; one person

volume—the amount of space that an object takes up

wicker—a strong but flexible material made from wood

Index

Let's Explore Math

Page 6:

a. 4 ft. × 6 ft. × 5 ft. = 120 cubic feet

b. 6 ft. × 8 ft. × 4 ft. = 192 cubic feet

Page 11:

78 m × 29 m × 53 m = 119,886 cubic meters

Page 15:

48 ft.^{3} ÷ (4 ft. × 3 ft.) = height

48 ft.^{3} ÷ 12 ft. = 4 ft. high

Page 19:

a. 4 ft. × 4 ft. × 5 ft. = 80 cubic feet

b. 1 person: 2 × 2 × 5 = 20 cubic feet;

80 cubic feet ÷ 20 cubic feet = 4

4 people can fit in the basket.

Page 22:

a. 8 m × 2 m × 3 m = 48 m^3

b. 48 m^3 × 1,000 L = 48,000 liters of water.

c. Answers will vary.

Page 27:

a. 2 m × 2 m × 4 m = 16 m^3

1 envelope is 16 m^3

b. volume of container:

8 m × 8 m × 2 m = 128 m^3

128 m^3 ÷ 16 m^3 = 8

8 balloons will fit in 1 container.

c. 8 balloon envelopes × 15 containers = 120

120 balloons will fit into 15 containers.

Problem-Solving Activity

a. Tank A: 6 ft. × 4 ft. × 5 ft. = 120 ft.^{3}

Tank B: 15 ft. × 4 ft. × 2 ft. = 120 ft.^{3}

b. Answers may vary, but should include the fact that Tank A and Tank B have the same volume, even though they have different dimensions.

c. 96 m^3 ÷ (8 m × 4 m) = 3 m

Tank C has a height of 3 meters.

d. 96 m^3 × 1,000 L = 96,000 L

Tank C holds 96,000 liters of water.